# I'M BETTER NOT BITTER

# I'M BETTER NOT BITTER

## My Personal Journey

## Kidney Transplant Recipient's Story of Winning in Business & Life and Moving Forward

## Anthony E. Tuggle

Achievement-oriented Senior Executive offering 20+ years of comprehensive business knowledge and hands-on experience in building productive teams and directing Fortune 10 Company project initiatives. Proven ability to effectively manage product and service delivery while leading commercial business service sales and care operations to ensure corporate growth and profit objectives.

During that time, he has acquired an extensive background in Consumer Sales & Service along with Customer Care and Sales Operations, Marketing, Product Management, Self Service / Ecommerce, and Product Development. He also has experience in Network Operations, Small Business, Human Resources, and Financial Management.

Anthony holds a Bachelor of Science in Psychology and a Master's Degree in Management. He is an Executive Education graduate of the University of North Carolina at Chapel Hill. In addition, Anthony graduated from Emory University's Executive MBA program in May 2014. Anthony actively participates in community events that support personal growth and development in others and efforts that have positively impacted the community. He is an active board member of the National Kidney Foundation and National Sales Network, advisory board member of Emory University Goizueta Business School and Board of Trustees at the Mount Vernon Presbyterian School.

An avid sports fan, he enjoys watching basketball and football. Anthony lives in Atlanta, Georgia, with his wife Nicole and their daughter Angelina.

I dedicate this book to God, my parents, my family and friends.

God, thank you for giving me your strength, wisdom, knowledge, power, health and wealth each and every day.

To my parents, thank you for instilling in me the attitude that I can do and accomplish anything I want to in life.

To wife and daughter, thank you for making me a better person!

To family and friends, thank you for believing in me unconditionally.

# Introduction

**"To whom much is given; much is expected"**

Inspiration from Luke 12:48

**"I'm winning even when they think I'm losing I'm winning"**

Anthony Tuggle

This book chronicles my personal journey dealing with my health, spiritual connection with God and my perspective on how to deal with "**Change**" and win at "**Life**." In addition, I share my key leadership learning's from my business experiences. This book is going to take you through a series of emotions. You are going to feel motivated, inspired, and ready to take on the world at the end of reading this book.

Repeat after me:

I will succeed

I won't give up

I can do anything

I must trust God

I believe in me

I win

I have won

# Contents

# Chapter 1

## My Journey Begins

## "It Takes a Village, No One Can Do It Alone"

Growing up in a large family of six, where my parents worked two jobs to ensure we had food on the table every night and clothing on our back so that we attended school every day. My parents never graduated from high school, therefore; education was very important to them. I was continuously told that you could do anything you set your mind to and to never allow anyone or anything to hold you back from your goals. My mother's number one priority was for her children to graduate from high school, and she reminded us of this constantly. She preached to us every day how important it was for us to complete high school, especially because they did not. My family frequently told me, especially my aunts that I would be successful and how proud they were of me.

As no surprise I was the first in my immediate family to graduate from college. In addition, my parents were successful in getting all of my siblings to graduate from high school. All my life I have carried the expectation and charge that I must be successful. I'm doing this for my parents, my family and me. I was fortunate to have a very strong support system from early childhood to adulthood. I'm so thankful for my parents and immediate/extended family: siblings, my aunts and uncles, cousins, etc. It was very clear to me early on that I must be successful and it was not optional. I vividly remember my aunts telling me "you are the one that we believe in and you will be successful." Even though it may seem small, it ultimately was a seed that stimulated growth and success. I learned at a young age that it's easy to concentrate on negativity and become pessimistic. The ability to recognize negative influences and keep a laser focus on the positive aspect of a situation is critical to my ability to remain optimistic in even the most difficult situation. I'm so thankful that my parents constantly reminded me that you are the chosen one in the family and we are all counting on you to be successful. I knew that they were depending on me and believed in me whole-heartedly, this was paramount for my success.

The story gets better; I was able to start a rewarding career in Corporate America. My journey involved moving eleven times across the United States, at least 20 different assignments and having an opportunity of a lifetime to work for a great company and grow both as an individual and leader. I am fortunate to know personally that these are blessings from God. I started my career as a Sales Representative and learned a long time ago "if you take care of your people they will take care of you". This valuable lesson has guided my actions throughout my career. People management is the most critical skill you can acquire as a leader.

My family, and friends, have always been the fuel for my journey. My father passed in 2007, and he taught me many valuable lessons. One key lesson was the fact that good things come to good people. My father was the heart of our family; he always jumped through hoops to make sure everyone in the family was taken care of. I remember many nights when family members would call our home because of some type of emergency and my father would get out of the bed late at night without hesitation to help them. He reinforced the importance of taking care of your family and friends and giving back to the community. My mother is a strong individual and a tough woman, if my father was the heart of our family; she has always been the backbone. Through her hard work and dedication, she demonstrated that it was possible to take on many things to take care of her family. She reinforced in me the belief that God will not place things on your plate that you cannot handle; this belief is at the foundation of who I am. My parents impressed upon me early that my mission in life is to give back to my family, friends and community and above all else to make a positive difference. This is table stakes to me and I believe this is my call to action to make a difference. My parents played an integral role in my journey and they provided me with the guidance, support, strength and prayer to take on the world. Now, I'm off to do great things and make them very proud!

# Chapter 2

## The Day God Spoke to Me "Worrying Doesn't Change the Outcome"

My belief is that everything happens for a reason; even bad things and you grow from all your experiences in life. For example, I was on my way achieving my goals both personally and professionally. I had a very successful career in Corporate America and things were on track as I planned. But as the saying goes "man plans, and God laughs", on January 15, 1998 I went to the doctor's office with what I thought was the flu. The doctor came in and I told him I had a common cold for the last couple of weeks that I couldn't seem to shake. I really needed something to help me get rid of this cold. The doctor examined me and ran some tests. I waited patiently for the doctor to return with the test results, while thinking about all the work that I had to do back at the office. I had been going to work every day for the last month with what I thought was a common cold. I had all of the symptoms of common cold; coughing, sneezing, fatigue, shortness of breath, body ache, etc. I was certain that I could shake it but after a month I realized that I needed to go to the doctor. When the doctor finally returned with my blood test results we had the most interesting exchange that I remember clearly, even today. It was almost an out of body experience; I understood everything he was saying but couldn't quite process why he was saying it to me. He started asking me a series of questions. "How long have you been sick?" I replied a couple of weeks. I asked him "what are you going to give me to address this cold?" Then, he asked, "How did you get here today? Did a family member or friend bring you into the office today?" I looked at him strangely and said, "No I drove myself and came here directly from work." He gave me a perplexed look and repeated my statement only as a question "you drove here yourself and you went to work today, also right?" I replied, "Yes sir, I have been going to work every day while fighting off this cold." I couldn't afford to miss a day because my team really needed me. At this point I started to get worried, and my internal dialogue kicked into overdrive. What is really wrong with me and why is the doctor asking me so many questions? As I fixed my posture with a very anxious look on my face, the doctor said: "Your blood pressure is extremely high, do you take any medicine for blood pressure?" I said no I'm not on any blood pressure medicine. He then said very interesting. "Have you not suffered from high blood pressure in the past?" I said I vaguely remember when I was younger experiencing lots of headaches and was told that my blood pressure was high but we never addressed it with medication. Now, I'm really getting scared and saying to myself "What did I do? What happen?" The doctor then replied, "Both of your kidneys have shut down, I'm not sure how you are able to walk into my office today much less how you are able to drive a vehicle and go to work." As I sat there with a very puzzled expression on my face I was silently praying "God please don't let me die staring at the doctor." Then the doctor commented in a matter of fact tone "you should have been dead." Of course, I'm now in a state of shock. I should be dead? What, this is crazy. I was at work today and drove to here. I'm must be dreaming; someone please wake me up as soon as possible. This is a bad dream, right? This is that point in your life when you realize this is some real stuff. You know I was using another word in my head at the time. Your life is about to change forever. The decisions you make from this point on will help shape the person you will become, this is one of those moments in time that you know that your life will never be the same. I needed to calm myself so that I could listen carefully to what the doctor was going to share next. The doctor went on to explain how serious my situation was, "we must place you on Dialysis immediately and you have to go to surgery to have a catheter place in your chest to facilitate the dialysis". My mind was racing and my head spinning. "Oh, my God! What is happening?" The doctor continued to explain that if I was not placed on Dialysis immediately I would die. That was when he informed me that I had end stage renal failure, which is Stage 5 kidney failure; my only options were dialysis or transplant. At the time, I had no idea what renal failure was and no clue about dialysis. This was almost 20 years ago, and we did not have a way to pull out our phone and "Google" it. This was a decision that I had to make right now. At first, I thought it was a decision that I had to make by myself. However, I could hear my mother's voice saying, "God doesn't put more on you than you can handle". At that moment I asked the doctor to give me a couple of minutes to get myself together. Also, the doctor didn't have the best bedside manners. Did this man just tell me that I should have been dead in a very matter of fact tone without any empathy? I guess he wanted to make sure I understand the seriousness of this illness. The doctor finally walked out and gave me some privacy. I immediately got on my knees and looked up to God and asked the following questions. "God, this is not how we are going to end my life right? I'm not ready to leave this world we have so much more to accomplish. We got this right?" And in my heart, I could hear God answer, "Yes we got this." I could still relive that important moment in time even today. I immediately jumped up and said out loud "we got this Lord." I asked the nurse to go get the doctor and to let him know I'm ready to go to surgery. The next important chapter of my life has just begun. At the time, I didn't know what was going to happen but I knew with confidence I was going to end on the right side.

# Chapter 3

# How To Handle Adversity aka Life Challenges (Dealing with Change) "Great Leaders Inspire Change"

On the path to greatness, having the courage to deal with adversity is fundamental. We know that change comes in many forms. It will impact us both professionally and personally. When things seem to be going against you, the ability to be agile in your reactions is paramount. Change is all about your perspective and we all know that it is inevitable. I know it's difficult but try not to fight it. The sooner you embrace change the better the outcome. It affords you the opportunity to avoid slowing down your growth during these turbulent times. The one thing most people forget when dealing with change is that growth is optional. Now, let me express how I utilized the emotions of change to deal with the devastating news that my kidneys had shut down and I had to go on dialysis immediately. I went through the following emotions during my doctor's visit: Shock, Anger, Resistance, Acceptance and Hope.

**Shock** is negatively dealing with the idea of change. I think shock is a nice way to say how I was truly feeling that day. I was probably more devastated. I was in a state of disbelief.  I keep saying to myself "I can't believe this is happening to me."

**Anger** is resentment and lots of skepticism set in. I was pissed off and mad at the world including god. I go to church regularly. I'm healthy; I never had to be admitted to a hospital. I was really frustrated with the doctor. He has to be wrong with his diagnosis. Let me take another blood test. You guys got this all incorrect.  "Well listen to what I heard... "I should be dead."

**Resistance** is feeling uncomfortable and want to keep everything status quo. There has to be some medication that the doctor can prescribe for me to take to avoid going on dialysis. "What are the other options?" I think we should monitor the situation over the next couple of days. "Why can't we get kidneys to function normally?"

**Acceptance** is starting to accept the fact that the change is happening. I think this may be the best solution. I really want to give this chance. I do not think I have any other course of action. "I think

Dialysis could work and give me a better quality of life."

**Hope** is excitement starting to build and a consideration around how to contribute to the change that is now under discussion. I believe I can go on Dialysis and still work and make strong influences in the community. "God has my back." I'm ready to make this next pivotal step in my life. "We can do this!"

These are the emotions of change that I experienced that day in the doctor's office. I know it's very surprising that a person can go through that many emotions during a short period of time. My ability to swiftly maneuver through these emotional stages set the foundation to receive blessings beyond my wildest dreams. I realized that these emotions are a natural reaction to tragic events. However, the ability to rebound with nimbleness reflects my relationship with God. Additionally, it promotes the capability to determine solutions efficiently. It's important that we learn from these changes and know that if we accept change it gets us closer to a positive outcome.

In my pursuit of greatness, the lesson I learned here is that we must adapt to change quickly and take every opportunity to inspire change to others.

# Chapter 4

## Dealing with Dialysis

## "Confidence is half the battle"

## "We are winning even when they think we are losing"

I was formally diagnosed with End State Renal Disease (ESRD) known as kidney failure. This is when your kidneys fail and stop working well enough for you to survive. The two options were dialysis, which was a short-term fix or a kidney transplant, the long game. ESRD is caused most commonly by diabetes and hypertension (high blood pressure). In my case, I arrived at the doctor office with high blood pressure this was thought to be a contributing factor to my kidney failure. Because I had ESRD I needed to go through hemodialysis commonly referred to as kidney dialysis or simply dialysis. Dialysis is a process of purifying the blood in effect doing the job of the non-functioning kidneys. I went to an outpatient dialysis facility in Atlanta, Ga. three times a week, Tuesday, Thursday and Saturday from 7am to 10am. The one thought that kept playing in my mind like a song stuck on repeat "Is this what I am going to be doing every Tuesday, Thursday and Saturday for the rest of my life?"

Now, it was time to decide whom I needed to tell about my diagnosis of end stage renal disease and the fact that I was going on dialysis. Of course, I told my parents and immediate family members right away and a very select group of friends. My decision to limit the number of people that knew about my situation was that I did not want anyone feeling sorry for me, and I certainly did not want to discuss my diagnosis or treatment every time I ran into them. I needed to stay focused and positive. Everyone is different and deals with challenges in their own way, this was the right decision and approach for me. At the time of my diagnosis my career was taking off, so I decided not to share this dramatic life changing news with my colleagues. I feared I would be judged and someone would decide on my career based on what they believed I could handle, I did not want anything to impact the trajectory of my career. I could not risk someone using this as an excuse for not giving me an opportunity or taking responsibilities of my plate. I decided to press through and buckle down so I could beat dialysis and get off of it quickly. During the first month of my dialysis treatments, I did a lot of research on kidney failure. I was determined to beat this disease. I learned that without life sustaining dialysis or a kidney transplant once an individual reaches end stage renal disease, toxins builds up in body and death usually comes within a few weeks. This was another mind-blowing moment with reality kicking in instantaneously.

I studied and found out that the "average life expectancy on dialysis is 5 – 10 years, however, many patients have lived well on dialysis for 20 or even 30 years." Clearly, my goal was to get off dialysis within a year or so and get a kidney transplant. I knew the road to recovery wouldn't be easy but "god didn't bring me this far to let me go." During dialysis, I read a lot of books to help me stay motivated; the bible was one book that I kept coming back to. I had determined early on that I would do my best to be an inspiration to the patients and nurses at the dialysis center. There was so much suffering and fear that we all needed to be reminded to focus on the positive. I had to relentlessly build my confidence up every day and continue to remind myself that "this is bigger than me, and God has a better plan for you." This became my daily affirmation "Take care of what counts, and God will take care of you." I started to get into an operating rhythm on the days I had dialysis, I would go to dialysis before heading to work. This was more than a routine this was survival. After eight months of dialysis treatment, I received a call at work that I was being promoted to Director. This was great news and I knew I had to take the job. I saw this as clear indication from God that I was on the right track. What was interesting about this opportunity was the fact that I had been a manager for the last 10 years, performed many roles in different parts of the company and moved several times but was unsuccessful in getting promoted to the next level. I packed my bags and moved to Kansas City, Mo. I had a lot of anxiety about the move because I was moving to a city where I had neither business contacts nor friends and had to find both a dialysis treatment center and a nephrologist. As I settled into my new location and new role at work I took the opportunity to reassess how much of my situation I should share and decided to continue to keep my diagnosis private and not share with anyone in my workplace. I simply explained to my team and assistant that every Tuesday and Thursday morning I had a personal commitment that I could not change and I would be in the office later on those days. I was called to conquer and knew if I stayed on my day-to-day operating rhythm and focus I would soon get to my goal. I moved to Kansas City in September of 1998, by February of 1999 I had settled in and created a small circle of friends that I felt comfortable enough with to share the information about my health.   I still did not tell anyone at work.

One of the books that helped me get through dialysis, which is now my favorite book: "Oh, the Places You'll Go! By Dr. Seuss." I believe this book is speaking directly to me. It starts off "Congratulations! Today is your day. You're off to Great Places! You're off and away! Oh! The Places You'll Go!" This is referencing going on dialysis in Atlanta, moving to Kansas City and getting a new promotion. Then the book goes on to say the following "You won't lag behind, because you'll have the speed. You'll pass the whole gang and you'll soon take the lead. Wherever you fly, you'll be the best of the best. Wherever you go, you will top all the rest." After being in Kansas City for six months, I received another call from my boss. And this time I couldn't believe the discussion. I knew this was a direct message from God and my praying parents sending me only positive thoughts regarding my situation. My boss shared with me that they were expanding my responsibility and I was being promoted to Executive Director. I waited ten years for a promotion and experienced a near death health tragedy. Because, I decided to take the leap of faith to transport through life without any regrets and not look back I have been promoted twice within twelve months or so. I'm going to end this chapter with the following insights from my favorite book: "And will you succeed? Yes! You will, indeed! (98 and ¾ percent guaranteed.) Kid, You'll Move Mountains!" So... be your name Anthony E Tuggle, "you're off to Great Places! Today is your day!

Your mountain is waiting. So... get on your way!"
This book reinforced my testimonies and all my
blessings. I'm on my way! Ready to take on the
world!

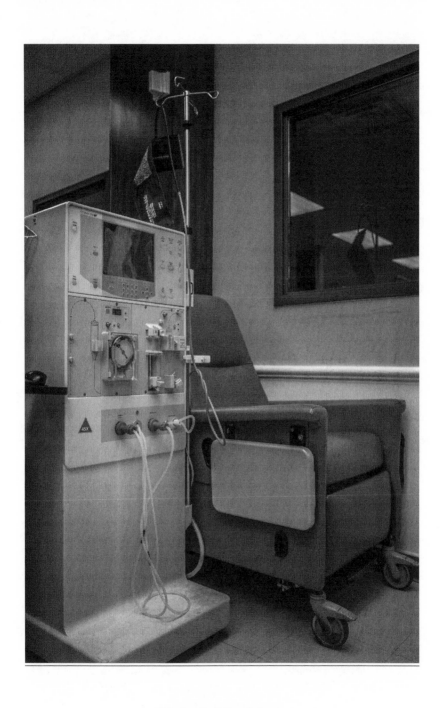

**Dialysis Machine**

# Chapter 5

## The Day My Life Changed
## "Always be Positive"
## (Optimism beats Pessimism every time)

Despite my health challenges things were going well for me in Kansas City, I had a great support system and wonderful friends. They have no idea what impact their relationship played on my ability to keep moving forward and staying positive. They reminded me that there are still some very good people living in this world. I still had not shared the news regarding my health issues with my work team and boss. Honestly, at this point it really didn't matter. I had a good process in place, very good staff at the dialysis center and an amazing nephrologist that provided the necessary care and support. Through their hard work, clear direction and my commitment to following their instructions to the letter I was successfully placed on the transplant list. Because in life you need to make sure you have every base covered my brothers were being tested to see if they were a match and could donate one of their kidneys to me.

Currently, there are approximately 100,000 people on the kidney transplant waiting list. The wait for a deceased donor could be 5 years, and in some states it is closer to 10 years. Patients are prioritized by how long they've been on the waiting list, their blood type, immune system activity and other factors." I did some research and based on the "American Journal of Transplantation in 1999 the wait list for kidney transplant was 41,000." You can clearly see that the list has doubled compared to the current statistics. I was very optimistic that I would eventually get that call telling me that they had a kidney ready for me. Or one of my brothers would call and say they were a match and can donate a kidney. I remained diligent and never missed a doctor's appointment or dialysis treatment and made sure I followed a healthy diet and stayed on top of my medications. I didn't want to miss this opportunity.

On May 5, 1999, it was a Wednesday and I still remember this day vividly. I was excited to hang out with my friends this evening and over the weekend to celebrate my birthday. Early that morning around 2am, I received a phone call from Emory University Hospital in Atlanta, Ga.

I had a lot of anxiety and my heart was racing, I said to myself "Is this the call I've been waiting for?" I picked up the phone and said "hello, hello, hello", the voice on the other end of the phone asked, "Is this Anthony Tuggle" and of course I said yes, this is Anthony. He went on to tell me "we have a kidney here in Atlanta waiting on you and it's a perfect match. You must get to Atlanta as soon as possible." I told him I would book the first flight out of Kansas City. I hung up the phone and literally had church in my town house. I just knew my neighbors were going to call the police; it was 2am in the morning but I didn't care. I got down on my knees and said "thank you God! You said you would take care of me as long as I stayed focus on the prize." Words cannot express the joy I felt that night. I am truly blessed! During the early morning I proceeded to make phone calls calling my parents, immediate family and friends. I also, called my direct reports and my boss. This was the right time for me to tell them about my situation, you can imagine the conversation that took place during those phone calls. I shared with them that I had been going to dialysis three times a week and had kidney failure. They were in a state of shock. But, I told them that I have better news now. I received a call from Emory University Hospital and they a kidney for me and I'm on my way to the airport to fly to Atlanta. I placed one of them in charge and told them I would call them after the surgery. Hallelujah!

"I'm on my way to Atlanta to get my kidney transplant!!!"

Today is my Birthday, what an amazing birthday present!

# Chapter 6

## My Birthday Is A National Holiday

## "You are in control of your own destiny"

I can't believe this day is finally here. Of course, I have not slept given the circumstances and the phone call I received this morning. I landed in Atlanta safely and now I'm at Emory University Hospital. I am going through so many emotions right now, all positive thoughts. I cannot wait to get this over and have my new kidney. The doctor came in and explained to me that I received a kidney from a deceased donor, which is called a cadaver. He informed me that he would be performing a cadaveric renal transplantation (kidney transplant). "Did I tell you that today was my birthday?" My family and friends are all at the hospital. Everyone is ready to celebrate my successful kidney transplant and my birthday. The room is full of joy and excitement. I owe all of this to God's grace and mercy in addition to the never wavering support of family and friends.

Around 2pm, on May 5th, my Birthday, I received my new kidney!!!! Yes!!!!!! I'm truly blessed!!!!!!
My Birthday is a National Holiday!!!!!!!!!

I'm full of so many emotions right now. This is an example that hard work, and dedication pays off. Let the celebration begin!

I will forever remember this day!

The journey has not been easy, living, as a kidney transplant recipient requires discipline and focus. To make sure that my new kidney remains healthy, I had to create a regiment that worked for me. The same discipline and determination that I used to propel my career, I now turned towards my physical health. There was no way that I was going to squander this amazing gift that I had been given.

After the Euphoria of getting a kidney wore off, I came to the realization that taking anti- rejection pills every day would be my reality for the rest of my life. I visited the nephrologist three to four times a year in the beginning and eventually these visits moved to every six months. In addition to the visits to my primary nephrologist, I visited the transplant center at Emory University Hospital once a year to ensure they continue to provide guidance and support on the progress of my transplant. Although I had the utmost of confidence in my doctors, my health was my responsibility. I paid close attention to all my test results and after 19 years I have become an expert of reading my lab reports. I stay in tune with my body and am very aware of signs or changes in my health, I do not hesitate to schedule an off cycle doctor's appointment based on signals from my body. This is now part of my daily regimen and I have a new appreciation for staying healthy. I maintain a healthy diet and try to exercise as regularly as possible. I've been doing this so long that it has become part of my lifestyle. "Your health matters" has become one of my new mantras; this will remain an important part of my life forever.

"My process for staying on top of my daily

pill regimen"

This experience has reinforced to me the importance of goal setting. The good news is that I've established personal goals for myself since 1994. This process has afforded me the opportunity to go back periodically throughout each year and assess the progress and validate whether I'm still on track and make the necessary changes. Successfully integrating these best practices have played an important role in this journey of life.

**"Setting goals are a good reference point of progress"**

It has been 19 years, and we are still celebrating this blessing from God. I have not had any rejections and remain in good physical and mental health. In addition, one of my closest friends is now my wife and we will be celebrating 14 years with our beautiful daughter. My wife has been the consistent rock and support throughout the last 20 years. I want to publicly say thanks for always being in my corner. I'm a better man and leader because of you!

You really do not know what obstacles you will face in life but you need to be ready to face them head on. I'm a witness that you can do anything you set your mind to. I'm off to continue to do great things in the world. Hopefully, my story has motivated you to go out and make a difference! Every year we celebrate my birthday as if it is 1999 and I just received my kidney transplant. This is a reminder that you are truly in control of your own destiny!

We are on our way to do great things!

My Birthday is a National Holiday!!!!!!

Currently, I sit on the National and Local Board of the National Kidney Foundation. Please join me in our fight to drive awareness and prevent chronic kidney disease. Please visit kidney.org for more information. There are many ways you can support this worthy cause.

Key Facts:

- 30 million American adults are estimated to have chronic kidney disease – and most aren't aware of it. In fact, 1 in 3 Americans is at risk.
- Kidney disease is the 9th leading cause of death in the U.S., and it is growing in prevalence.
- Risk factors for kidney disease include diabetes, high blood pressure, heart disease, obesity and family history of kidney failure.
- When your kidneys stop working, so do you. National Kidney Foundation is working to elevate knowledge about, and concern for, kidneys to the level of the body's other organs such as heart.
- Nearly, 100,000 Americans are waiting on a kidney transplant right now. Whether you need a kidney or are considering living donation, let NKF help you start the conversation. Visit kidney.org/livingdonation or call 855-NKF-CARES for free resources and support through THE BIG ASK: THE BIG GIVE.

# Chapter 7

## MY MVP – Mission, Vision, and Purpose

### "Greatness requires being Detail Oriented and having Operating Rhythm"

Every successful leader must have a plan, strategy, value statement, belief or what some would call a mantra to best represent them and serve as a motivation to whom they are and what they want to accomplish out of life. This mantra will help people identify with them and hopefully make a connection. This is about giving people something to believe in to make a difference. I believe deep down everyone wants to make some type of difference in the world. Let me say this, I hope so anyway. Hope gives us the ability to believe that something great can really happen. It serves, as a motivation to inspire us to do the things that most say cannot to be accomplished. Hope allows us to trust the process and people. Hope means you are capable of having a positive outlook on your current situation. I think we need hope to believe in each other and to make the world a better place to live. A lot of times people do not want to talk about hope but those are some of the best conversations you can have with one another. It forces us to think about the impossible and walk away with some valuable lesson learned. We must continue to be open to allow the positive energy to come into our lives and not try to criticize it or deny it from the beginning. It's ok to believe in something so strongly and rally behind it to make a difference in our day-to-day lives. Now that I have your attention let's talk about my mantra. First, let me take the time to define what a mantra is, since there are many different perceptions out there. It's important to me that we are on the same page. A mantra is usually any repeated word or phrase, but it can also refer more specifically to a word repeated in meditation. It's a positive phrase or affirmation that you say to yourself for the purpose of motivation or encouragement. My mantra is my MVP. It's my mission, vision and purpose. The mission is what drives you and should inspire and motivate you each and every day. The vision is where you aspire to be in life. This is what you want to be in the future. The purpose is what guides you. This is why you do what you want to do and what you are passionate about in life. The MVP has played an integral role in shaping me as a leader. The best part of this model is that it can be applied to both my personal and business life. It is instrumental to my ability to accomplish my goals. The MVP represents who I am as a person. It's how I want people to evaluate my accomplishments and me.

**My mission** is to make people around me "Great". I want to teach people how to win in both their personal and business life I want to be a life coach to others. I want others to learn from my mistakes or failures in life. I believe we must fail fast. We grow from our failures. If we do not celebrate our shortcomings we reduce our ability to grow under any circumstances. I want to teach people how to win and be the best individual they can be in life. **My vision** is that I want to make an impact in my community. This is about making a strong contribution that makes a difference. I want to lead people through the storm. I do not give up. I'm relentless and I move forward because this is what it takes to make an impact under all situations.

**My purpose** is about giving back to others, my family, friends, colleagues and communities. God gave me a second chance. I think we only get one opportunity and if we are lucky, to make a difference. In my case, I do not believe in luck and I prefer not to offend anyone but I'm not lucky, I'm blessed. God keeping me here was an opportunity for me to make a difference. I have accepted the calling from God and my role to go out and share my blessing with others. This should be easy for me because he gave me another chance at life.

I hope my MVP can serve as a guide to help you get closer to your dreams and goals. This is a good framework for you to easily simplify your key deliverables. My hope is that everyone will take the time to develop your own mission, vision and purpose. This template can be used at home with your significant other and family and at work with your boss, colleagues and team. Please keep these three things in mind as you grow in your career. Also, your MVP will evolve over time based on your life experiences. So, what's stopping you from being a Great Leader in your personal and business life and in your community?  Let's go do great things in the world. My call to action is that everyone takes the necessary time to complete his or her personal MVP.

# What's Your MVP?

**Mission**
*drives* you

- Your *mission statement* is what you do to accomplish your goals - the difference you will make and what change will happen
- It should inspire and motivate you each and every day

**Vision**
is where you
*aspire* to be

- Your *vision statement* is where you will be in the future and the results you want to achieve

**Purpose**
*guides* you

- Your *purpose statement* is why you do what you do and the cause you are passionate about
- This should highlight your values and what makes up your character

# Chapter 8

**The Impact of Tuggle Nation "Win the Hearts and Minds" "If you take care of your people they will take care of you"**

As a leader, my ultimate goal is to create a culture where everyone can win and make strong contributions. This is about building an environment where employees want to come to work each and every day and will recommend their family and friends to do business with their employer. The employees take pride in where they work. They are proud of the workplace. I believe that people management is the single most impactful skill you can learn as a manager and leader. I learned early in my career, as a sales representative and team manager, that if you take care of your people they will take care of you. In addition, it is so important to treat all individuals with the same respect you want to be treated, especially in a work environment. If you treat employees like adults, this will accelerate your chances of being a successful team. Leaders that perform these types of initiatives will develop best in class teams or groups and deliver world-class results. These best practices are not difficult to implement. They require managers and leaders to put in the appropriate amount of work and commitment to doing the right thing for the organization. At the end of the day, this is about "winning the hearts and minds" and giving employees something that they can believe in and rally behind. It provides a sense of unity and one team concept. We win together!

Now let's talk about Tuggle Nation. Tuggle Nation is what my group of employees and vendors call themselves at work. It is often referred to as a family. There is even some water cooler talks from other groups for 'kicks and giggles' calling us a cult. We are a group that has built a strong foundation of trust, open communication, support for each other, a desire to win and be the best in the industry. People always ask, "How did you guys determine the name of the group?" The name originated during one of my Town Hall meetings several years ago. Tuggle Nation is more than a name; it is a movement that grew organically after its introduction at that Town Hall meeting. This is something that you cannot orchestrate, it is a good example of how grassroots efforts can develop and spread across an entire organization. Tuggle Nation took off very rapidly and has built a strong brand across the company to my surprise. This is evidence that when you create a culture with high employee engagement and believe in them unconditionally they will do amazing things. As I sit here today, and reflect on Tuggle Nation, I have so much humility, thankfulness and gratitude to be leading a group that is so passionate about winning, taking care of customers and being the best in the marketplace.

Keeping your finger on the pulse of your organization, and staying in tune with your employees is critical to continued success. Conducting employee surveys and learning from our employees is a vital part of our model. We consistently poll the organization to get a pulse around best practices and key learning's from the group.

Here are some of the common themes:

- A Positive culture drives high productivity and results
- Winning the hearts and minds is essential
- Clear and transparent communication is fundamental
- Winning together and teamwork is not optional
- Adapt quickly and fail fast
- Employee engagement is critical
- Strong brand, positive attitude and family environment
- Take care of your people, they will take care of you

Win the hearts and minds of your people   WIN!   Self-development

Try and fail fast, but try!   Strive for success   P.I.E. Performance, Image, Exposure   Work hard, play hard

Make it happen   Execute well   Career Development   Be focused, determined, and straight forward

Build a winning culture   Pay attention to details   Learn from your failures   It all starts with me

Take care of our people   Tuggle Nation is a family   Fail fast   Adapt quickly

Never stop developing your skills   Win and have fun doing so

Find a way   Social media   Thank your people   Drive strong results   Perform without excuses

Performance, Image, and Exposure   Win the hearts and minds of our people

Make it happen   Continue educating yourself   Inspire and motivate

Being balanced   Build your personal brand   Great leaders find a way to win

Engaged   Win, Win, Win!   Create a winning culture   Think fast on your feet

Invest in your future   Be flexible   You can decide to take charge of your career   Keep the team updated and aligned

Excellence is the expectation   Employee engagement is more than a metric

Get outside comfort zone

Transparency   Display a confidence that we have the best team   Connect with your people

Open and honest communication   Develop your brand   Relentless pursuit of excellence

Personal development

Pivot quickly   Win together   Champion change   Constant communication

Put your people first   Appreciate your people

Change is a critical part of the job

60

Tuggle Nation is the result of creating an environment where everyone can win and make strong contributions. Most people want to be on a winning team; they are ultimately normally looking for something to believe in. Connecting with your frontline employees and vendors is critical, and there is no shortcut, you have to be willing to put in the work necessary to make the connection. This is about giving back and making a difference in people's lives. Tuggle Nation has created an opportunity for people to live out their dreams and make a strong contribution back to their families and communities.

**"Winning the hearts and minds"**

# Chapter 9

# Authentic Leadership
# "Embrace Being Different"

Most authentic leaders build their brands based on their honest and trustworthiness relationships with their employees, followers, groups and organization that value their input and ethical foundations. Authentic leaders are defined as self-aware and genuine. They are normally aware of their strengths, their limitations, and their emotions and do not make excuses for their style and approach. They have a tendency to show their real selves and personality to their followers in all settings. They are normally referred to as the "real deal."

Authentic leaders are not afraid to be who they are at all times. They are very comfortable being themselves.

Throughout my career, during the early stages of being an executive in Corporate America, I often struggle with allowing my true authentic self to be visible all the time in the workplace. I received a lot of feedback about not being like everyone else. I have a very different leadership style and I'm very passionate about my employees and my business. People would often misconstrue my passion, for anger, in interactions where I was never upset. My communication style is very transparent, direct and influential. What they didn't realize was that I was operating on a different time line of life. As I shared earlier, I only started sharing with my extended family, friends and colleagues about my kidney transplant over the last couple of years. I did not want people to feel sorry for me nor make this part of our everyday conversation. In addition, I did not want people to hold this against for some reason. I had enough things they were already questioning and holding against me. As I look back over my career and life, I wish I had shared it sooner. However, I was not ready to start sharing my personal experiences publicly. With the help of god, a strong wife, praying and supportive family and friends, I able to keep pushing forward and worked really hard to be the best in my industry. I learned a long time ago to never look back and start questioning things that happen to you in the past. The best life lesson for me was we grow as a leader from our failures, mistakes and uncomfortable situations and events of life. I'm a better person in all aspects of my life because of all of my experiences.

Over the last several years, I started to become more and more of my true authentic leader.  I realize that it was okay for me to be me. Honestly, I must thank Tuggle Nation for reinforcing to me that they loved me the way I am. Also, they reminded me that I was a great leader and a jewel to them. I can't believe I'm sharing this publicly but this is part of the healing and growing process for me. This should remind us all,  to never allow anyone to place limitations on your capabilities and you can do anything you set your mind to. As my parents told me many days and nights, I can honestly say they were damn right!  I know that my calling in life is bigger than any title or job.  I must get this message out to the masses in hope that if I change one person's life I have succeeded. I hope you have a better understanding now why I'm so passionate about life. I was given a second chance to do some amazing things for some incredible deserving people. I do not want to leave this wonderful world with any regrets. I take what I do very seriously and at the end of the day all I want to be is great and make a difference. I would encourage all of you to tell your story and embrace being different from the norm.

Lastly, I play three roles: teacher, boss and leader.

**As a Teacher**, I teach people how to win in life and business.

**As a Boss**, I make the tough decisions and not afraid to do so.

**As a Leader**, I lead people over the goal line. I do not give up.

My name is Anthony E Tuggle and I'm a proud Authentic Leader!

Here are my 10 attributes of Authentic Leadership:

1. You are Ok with being you
2. You realize it's bigger than you
3. You make time for what's important
4. You don't forget where you started from
5. Your actions mirror your words
6. You aren't afraid to be vulnerable
7. You put others before you
8. You have a clear sense of integrity
9. You know it's not all about you
10. You know you cannot do it all on your own

# Conclusion

## I'm Better Not I'm Bitter

## "A Setback is a Setup for a

## Comeback"

In closing, writing this book was very therapeutic for me. I'm not use to being vulnerable. My family, friends and colleagues normally call me "Superman." I do not normally share my personal perspective with anyone. I spent the last twenty years not sharing with many people my diagnosis of kidney disease and the fact that I had a kidney transplant 19 years ago. I recently shared these health challenges with close friends and colleagues. This was very hard for me to share. I did not want to people to feel sorry for me. I did not want people to make excuses to stop me from achieving my goals and becoming successful. There are so many reasons why people could come up with justifications as to why I should not be where I am today. However, I prefer not to focus on the negative and as Michelle Obama stated, "When they go low we go high." We never want to allow enemies to have leverage or steer us away from our ultimate goal.

Please listen carefully; this is an important life lesson. "A setback is a setup for a comeback!" We will all have setbacks; it's how you respond to them? My experiences did not make me bitter; they made me better. At any given time, I could have given up and thrown in the towel. I did not make any excuses and quickly accepted the challenge and paved a way with great family and friends by my side to move forward.

Are you ready to go do great things? Are you truly ready to go do great things? This is our time and if not now when? I believe in you 100%! You can do anything you set your mind to do. The only person standing in the way of your blessings is you. Now, let's go do great things and make us all proud!

My name is Anthony E Tuggle and "I'm Better and not Bitter."

# Glossary of Tuggle-isms

**My philosophies based on my experiences in business and life**

1. "The Importance of having operating rhythm and being organized"
2. "A person is only as valuable as their word"
3. "People make time for what is important"
4. "Confidence is half the battle; We are winning even when they think we are losing"
5. "Express how you feel, it promotes a clear mind (which is important for progress)"
6. "Don't forget to give yourself some credit"
7. "You are in control of your own destiny"
8. "Worrying doesn't change the outcome"
9. "Greatness requires being detail oriented"
10. "Win the Hearts and Minds"

11. "Preparation is a powerful tool (especially when the haters will try to trip you up)"
12. "Great Leaders inspire change"
13. "High Standards separate you from the masses"

14. "Persistence is key (Don't accept no for an answer)"
15. "Adopting positive habits are a necessary challenge"
16. "If you take care of your people they will take care of you; good bosses listen more than they speak"
17. "Take accountability for your own actions"
18. "Thorough communication is powerful and needed in both business and life"
19. "It takes a village...no one can do it alone"
20. "Embrace being different"
21. "Always be positive (optimism beats pessimism every time)"

22. "Good physical health and mental health are both very important"

23. "A Setback is a Set up for a Comeback"

24. "Challenge yourself (be your biggest critic)"

25. "Last but not least...always appreciate the little things"

# "The importance of having operating rhythm and being organized"

Good organizational skills can help reduce stress and save time. This means being able to balance many tasks in your life or business efficiently and effectively. We need operating rhythm to drive consistency and order. It allows you to create a structure that can be easily followed. It's a key element to be successful.

## "A person is only as valuable as their word"

A person's word is his bond. When you make a promise, you keep it.
This is a reflection of your character. People will evaluate you based on your word and action and did you keep your commitment to others.  This is so vital to any relationship business or personal and a must for leading large teams, groups or organizations.

# "People make time for what is important"

Time management is key. We are all very
busy with our day-to-day lives
balancing work, family and friends. It is so
easy to not have enough time
to squeeze everyone into our schedule.
However, when it's really important to us
we will make it work and find the time.
Make it a priority and you will find the time.

# "Confidence is half the battle; we are winning even when they think we are losing"

An important trait in believing in you is having the confidence. Being confident gives you the motivation needed to get up and keep fighting no matter what you are dealing with in life. You cannot win without having confidence and truly believing that you can conquer the goal.

# "Express how you feel, it promotes a clear mind (which is important for progress)"

Being able to express your true feelings to others openly will play a vital role in your progress. This is part of your self-development. You cannot fully grow as an individual or leader until you are able to articulate your true feelings.

# "Don't forget to give yourself credit"

One of the biggest mistakes we make is not taking the time to pat ourselves on the back. We are so critical of oneself that it is easy to forget that we need encouragement as well. We must learn how to become our own cheerleader at times when we need it the most. This will prepares us to be ready to take on life challenges.

# "You are in control of your own destiny"

This is about leading and living the best life for you. You must know your self worth. You are the only one that can steer your life in the right direction. This is about believing and trusting in you.

# "Worrying doesn't change the outcome"

We tend to spend a lot of time worrying about things out of our control. This is a waste of energy and negative thoughts. We need to focus on the things within our control that our actions can determine the best outcomes. This will ensure we are mentality ready to take on the challenge and deal with adversity.

# "Greatness requires being detail oriented"

Being great comes with the highest level of expectation. Therefore, you must sweat the details. You have to "inspect what you expect". You are required to role model the necessary behaviors needed for your teams. You are striving to be the "best of the best".

# "Win the Hearts and Minds"

This is about creating an environment when everyone can win and be successful. Everybody wants to be on a winning team. We all want to be part of something special that we can believe in. This is a culture where we have common ground, values, beliefs, and goals and operate as one team. This will result in the highest level of employee engagement.

# "Preparation is a powerful tool especially when the haters will try to trip you up"

Being prepared for mostly every situation is key. Preparation is about expecting the unexpected and knowing how to react to them. Planning in advance is crucial and having back up plans are vital for success. You must learn how to be relentless in your pursuit of preparation.

# "Great Leaders Inspire Change"

Change comes in many forms; personally and professionally. Change is Inevitable and Growth is Optional. This is about your perspective. Don't fight change – Embrace it! Remember, Good Leaders Adapt to Change and Great Leaders Inspire Change. It only takes you to change your life!

# "High Standards separate you from the masses"

Don't be afraid to have high standards and expect excellence all the time. We spend a lot of time at work away from our families. If you are going to work this hard and put in many long hours at the office, you should want to be the best of the best. Don't make excuses for holding people accountable and teaching them how to win.

## "Persistence is key (Don't accept no for an answer)"

This is about not giving up. Stay focus on your dreams and goals. It is so easy to give up but much harder to keep pushing forward. Your hard work will payoff. Please trust the process. You must stay committed to the grind and day to day hustle. You will win at the end. Determination is the key to Persistence.

# "Adopting positive habits are a necessary challenge"

Doing repetitive positive things over and over again will always likely turn out a very positive outcome. However, we must constantly challenge ourselves to find ways to stay positive. It is so easy to adopt negative habits.  In order to adopt positive habits you must have a desire to change, consistent effort, time and commitment.

## "If you take care of your people they will take care of you; good bosses listen more than they speak"

People management is the most important skill you can learn as a leader. Taking care of your people should be your top priority. You must treat them like adults and with the same level of respect you want to be treated at all time. Always explain why something is happening or taking place. Never assume they know the outcome of any situation.

# "Take accountability for your own actions"

Always take ownership for your actions. Never make excuses and blame others. It is always easier to point the finger towards someone else. Remember when you are accountable you are building trust that could last a lifetime.

## "Thorough communication is powerful and needed in both business and life"

Communications sometimes get lost in translation. Therefore, you must make sure you are clear, concise and transparent in all your interactions. Remember, it is very important to listen first and seek understanding before responding to any situation. Always keep in mind and consider how you are delivering your message as well.

# "It takes a village...no one can do it alone"

We all need help from someone to succeed. Please do not be naïve and think you can do everything without anyone. It's ok to accept help from family, friends and colleagues who you love and trust. They actually would love to help you conquer your goals and dreams. Remember to create that environment where people can easily provide assistance to you during those tough times.

## "Embrace being different"

We want you to be authentic. We want you to be proud of who you are and willing to share the whole you with us. It's ok for you to be you. You should tell your story! We all have a story to tell.

# "Always be Positive (Optimism beats Pessimism every time)"

We all enjoy being around positive people. Positive people brighten up the room. You look forward to seeing them every day. It helps when you can find the positive in mostly any given situation. Being positive helps your mental state as well. It doesn't cost you anything to have a positive outlook on life.

# "Good Physical Health and Mental Health are both very important"

This is about making the right lifestyle changes in our lives. Your mental state is as important as your physical health. We need to think about them both together and not separately. They both play a huge role in reducing stress and how we deal with life obstacles. Please remember your overall health matters.

# "A Setback is a Setup for a Comeback"

We will all have setbacks; it's how we respond to them. We grow from our experiences. How we deal with adversity is the key. Remember, we determine the outcome of these situations. We got this!

# "Challenge Yourself (be your biggest critic)"

This is about your self-awareness and development. You should only be competing with yourself and against your own personal goals. This is about you becoming a better you.  This should be your ultimate journey making you great!

# "Last but not least…always appreciate the little things"

Life is way too short and time is moving way too fast. Please take the time to celebrate the small things. These are the things that matter the most to us and our family, friends and colleagues. You do not want to leave this wonderful place with any regrets. The time is now and do not wait until tomorrow. Let's go celebrate all the tiny things and small wins in our life.